Crafts for Kids Who Are
LEARNING ABOUT
TRANSPORTATION

KATHY ROSS
Illustrated by Jan Barger

ML Millbrook Press

Minneapolis

To Greyson, who is going places.

Text copyright © 2007 by Kathy Ross

Illustrations copyright © 2007 by Millbrook Press, Inc.

Millbrook Press, Inc.
A division of Lerner Publishing Group
241 First Avenue North
Minneapolis, Minnesota 55401 U.S.A.

Website address: www.lernerbooks.com

Library of Congress Cataloging-in-Publication Data

Ross, Kathy (Katharine Reynolds), 1948–
    Crafts for kids who are learning about transportation / by Kathy Ross ;
  illustrated by Jan Barger.
      p.   cm. — (Crafts for kids who are learning about...)
    ISBN-13: 978–0–7613–9464–8 (lib. bdg. : alk. paper)
    ISBN-10: 0–7613–9464–8 (lib. bdg. : alk. paper)
    1. Handicraft—Juvenile literature. 2. Transportation in art—Juvenile
  literature. I. Barger, Jan, 1948– II. Title.
  TT160.R7127 2007
  745.5—dc22   2005016461

Manufactured in the United States of America
1 2 3 4 5 6 – JR – 12 11 10 09 08 07

Table of Contents

Baby Carriage Photo Frame

Here is what you need:

cardboard egg carton

trim

four identical small buttons

6-inch (15-cm) pipe cleaner

photograph of you as a baby

white craft glue

fabric scrap

scissors

cotton ball

ruler

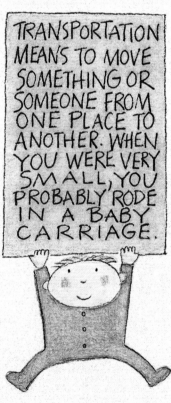

TRANSPORTATION MEANS TO MOVE SOMETHING OR SOMEONE FROM ONE PLACE TO ANOTHER. WHEN YOU WERE VERY SMALL, YOU PROBABLY RODE IN A BABY CARRIAGE.

Here is what you do:

1. Cut two cups from the cardboard egg carton.

2. Turn one cup sideways, and glue it in one end of the second cup to form the baby carriage.

3. Glue the four buttons around the bottom of the carriage for the wheels.

4. Glue trim around the top edge of the carriage and around the carriage shade to decorate.

5. Cut a 3-inch (8-cm) square of fabric. Wrap the fabric around the cotton ball, and glue it into the carriage to look like a blanket.

6. Cut the head from an old baby photograph, and tuck the bottom under the blanket at the head of the carriage.

7. Cut a 5-inch (13-cm) piece of the pipe cleaner.

8. Fold the pipe cleaner into a U shape. Slide the ends into the carriage at the point where the hood tucks inside the carriage base.

Be sure to ask your grown-up before cutting up any old photographs. The grown-up might want to make a copy for you to use instead.

Wagon Skill Puzzle

Here is what you need:

three different colors
of craft foam

clear plastic from a
blister pack, such as
batteries come in

two small beads

thin ribbon
or trim

scissors

black permanent
marker

white craft glue

hole punch

HAVE YOU
EVER BEEN
PULLED
AROUND
IN A
WAGON?

Here is what you do:

1. Cut two squares of craft foam the same size as the outer edge of the clear plastic.

2. Cut a small rectangle from the third color of craft foam for the wagon.

3. Glue the wagon to one of the foam squares.

4. Use the marker to draw a handle for the wagon.

5. Use the hole punch to punch two holes below the wagon where the wheels should be.

6. Glue the second craft foam square behind the first square with the wagon on it.

7. Squeeze glue around the edges of the foam.

8. Carefully set the two beads in the holes, and then set the plastic over the wagon. Do not move the puzzle until the glue has dried, or the beads will go to the edge and get stuck in the glue.

9. Glue ribbon or trim around the outside of the puzzle to give it a finished look.

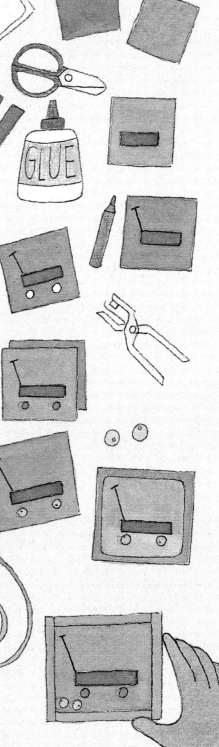

To play with the skill puzzle, try to shake the two beads into the holes to give the wagon wheels.

Bike Bobber

Here is what you need:

small round balloon

milk cap

1½-inch (3.8-cm) Styrofoam ball

12-inch (30-cm) sparkle stem

small red and blue ball-top pins

scissors

three craft beads

thin ribbon

AS YOU GET OLDER, YOU CAN MOVE YOURSELF AROUND ON A TRICYCLE AND THEN A BICYCLE.

Here is what you do:

1. Cut off most of the neck of the balloon.

2. Slip the balloon over the Styrofoam ball to cover it.

3. Use ball-top pins to attach the beads to the ball for eyes and a nose.

4. Use red ball-top pins to shape a smile on the Styrofoam ball.

5. Attach the milk cap to the top of the ball with a ball-top pin to make a hat.

6. Wrap the sparkle stem around your finger to make a spiral. Push one end of the sparkle stem up into the Styrofoam ball through the opening at the neck of the balloon.

7. Tie the neck of the balloon shut with a 6-inch (15-cm) piece of the ribbon tied into a bow.

Wrap the bottom end of the sparkle stem around the handlebar of your tricycle, and watch the bobber bob and bow as you pedal along.

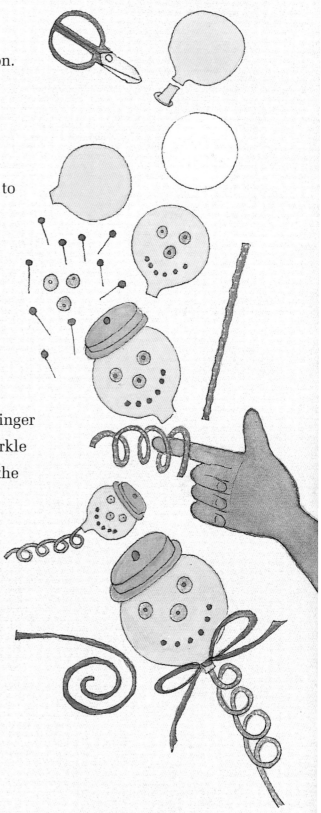

Doll Friend Saucer

Here is what you need:

9-inch (23-cm)
Styrofoam plate

small hole punch

four 12-inch (30-cm)
pipe cleaners

rubber band

string

ruler

scissors

clear packing tape

IF THERE IS SNOW
WHERE YOU LIVE,
YOU CAN TAKE A
RIDE ON A SLED
OR A SAUCER.

Here is what you do:

1. Make a handle on each side of the plate by cutting a piece from the rim that is 2 inches (5 cm) long and 1 inch (2.5 cm) wide.

2. Wrap two of the pipe cleaners around the outer edge of the handles. Trim off any extra pipe cleaner left after each handle is covered.

3. Cut a 24-inch (61-cm) length of string for the rope pull for the saucer.

4. Punch two holes in the edge of the saucer about 5 inches (13 cm) apart.

5. Thread the two ends of the string up through the two holes from the bottom. Knot the ends of the string together to make the rope pull.

6. Use the packing tape to secure one side of the rubber band to the center of the saucer to make a "seat belt" to hold your doll or animal friend in place.

If you haven't got a snowy hill to slide the saucer down, try sliding it down a long piece of cardboard propped up on one end to make a slanted surface.

Horse and Rider

Here is what you need:

three clamp clothespins

photo of you

two wooden spoons

two large black seed beads

scrap of brown construction paper

scissors

blue and brown poster paint and a paintbrush

black yarn

Styrofoam tray to work on

white craft glue

GLUE

two small wiggle eyes

ruler

ANIMALS CAN HELP PEOPLE MOVE FROM PLACE TO PLACE.

Here is what you do:

1. Clamp two of the clothespins to one of the wooden spoons about 1 inch (2.5 cm) from each end to create the body for the horse. Secure with glue.

2. Glue the second wooden spoon to the small end of the body spoon, handle end down, for the head.

3. Cut two ears for the horse from the brown construction paper. Glue the ears to the top of the head.

4. Paint the horse brown, and let it dry on the Styrofoam tray.

5. Paint the second clothespin blue, and let it dry on the Styrofoam tray.

6. Glue the two wiggle eyes to the head below the horse's ears. Glue the two seed beads to the bottom end of the head for nostrils.

7. Glue some black yarn bits between the ears for the forelock of the horse.

8. Cut five 4-inch (10-cm) pieces of black yarn for the tail. Knot the pieces together at one end. Glue the knotted end to the back of the horse.

9. Cut around a photo of you from the waist up. Clip the clothespin to the horse. Glue the photo to the top of one side of the clothespin so the handles look like legs coming down from the photo.

Rest the clothespin rider on the horse. Giddyap!

Honking Car

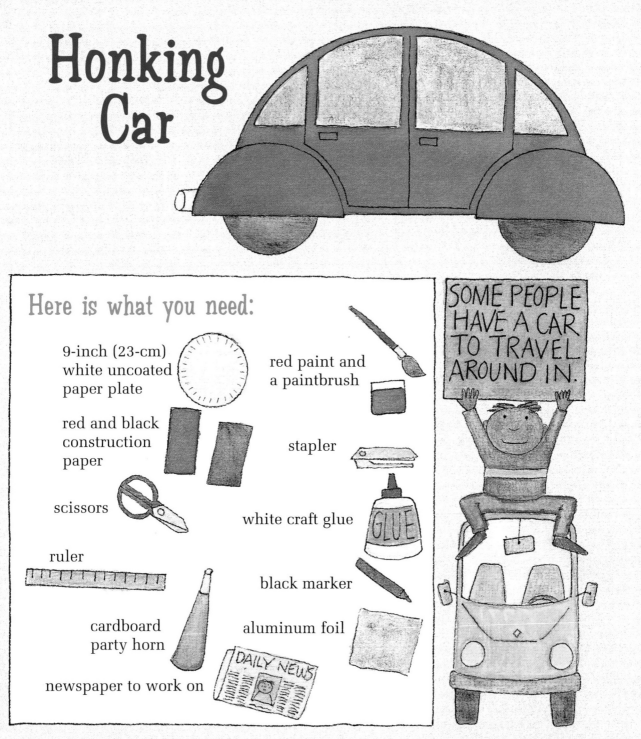

Here is what you need:

- 9-inch (23-cm) white uncoated paper plate
- red and black construction paper
- scissors
- ruler
- cardboard party horn
- newspaper to work on
- red paint and a paintbrush
- stapler
- white craft glue
- black marker
- aluminum foil

SOME PEOPLE HAVE A CAR TO TRAVEL AROUND IN.

Here is what you do:

1. Working on newspaper, paint the bottom of the paper plate red and let it dry.

2. Fold the painted plate in half around the party horn so that the mouthpiece of the horn sticks out of one end of the fold. The red side of the plate should be on the outside. Staple around the edge of the plate to secure. This will be the body of the car.

3. Cut a 4-inch (10-cm) circle from the red construction paper. Cut the circle in half to make the two fenders for the car.

4. Cut two 2-inch (5-cm) circles from the black construction paper for the wheels of the car.

5. Glue the flat end of a fender to the top of each wheel.

6. Glue a fender and a wheel to each end of the folded plate so that about half of each fender sticks out at the front and back of the car.

7. Use the marker to draw doors on the car.

8. Cut windows and the back and front windshields of the car from the aluminum foil. Glue the windows and windshields in place on the car.

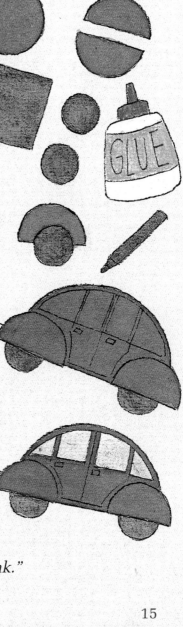

Blow on the party horn mouthpiece to make the car "honk."

Race Car Photo Holder

Here is what you need:

two wooden craft sticks

wooden clamp clothespin

photo to use for driver

poster paint and a paintbrush

white craft glue

Styrofoam tray to work on

metallic trim

scissors

six craft jewels

GLUE

SOMETIMES PEOPLE MAKE A GAME OUT OF SEEING WHO CAN TRAVEL THE FASTEST. HAVE YOU EVER SEEN A CAR RACE?

Here is what you do:

1. Glue a craft stick on each side of the clamp clothespin so that the handles of the clothespin stick up on each side for fins at the back of the car.

2. Paint the car, and let it dry on the Styrofoam tray.

3. Glue a craft jewel to the inside front and back sections of the car on each side, silver side out, to make the wheels.

4. Glue two craft jewels to the front of the car for the headlights.

5. Decorate each side of the car by gluing on a strip of metallic trim.

6. Cut around the head of a photo. Clamp the bottom of the photo in the clothespin to become the driver for the car.

You can use a photo of yourself or someone else for this project or cut a favorite race car driver from a magazine to use as the driver for your car. If you use a magazine picture, glue the head to construction paper to give it a stiff backing. Cut around the head, and clamp it into the car. Beep! Beep!

Police Car Chasing Getaway Car

Here is what you need:

three strong craft
magnet discs

a red and a blue ¾-inch (2-cm)
stationery sticker dot

four black and
one red large-size
seed beads

white craft glue

black ballpoint pen

SPECIAL KINDS OF VEHICLES ARE USED FOR DIFFERENT JOBS.

Here is what you do:

1. Use the pen to draw the side view of a police car on the blue stationery dot and a car on the red stationery dot. They should both be facing the same direction.

2. Stick two of the magnets together.

3. Hold the two magnets beside the third magnet to find which side of the two magnets pushes the single magnet away.

4. Stick the red car on the single magnet and the blue police car on the double magnet so that the front of the police car will push the back of the getaway car away.

5. Glue two black seed beads at the bottom of each car for the tires.

6. Glue the red seed bead to the top of the police car for the red light.

Place the two cars on a smooth surface, and the police car will "chase" the getaway car.

Human Bulldozer

Here is what you need:

12- by 16-inch (30- by 40-cm) low carton such as canned goods come in

18-ounce size (510-g) oatmeal box

scissors

white craft glue

A BULLDOZER IS USED TO MOVE BIG PILES OF DIRT OR DEBRIS.

Here is what you do:

1. Cut the rim off of the carton. Cut off one short end of the rim. Trim the two long sides to about 14 inches (36 cm).

2. Cut the bottom out of the oatmeal box. Cut the box in half.

3. Glue the two halves, one inside the other, together to make the bulldozer scoop.

4. Glue the scoop to the short side of the carton rim.

5. To use, hold onto the two loose ends of the carton rim and push the scoop along the floor to move debris into a pile. You might try moving different items such as crumpled paper, blocks, or cotton balls.

Maybe a handheld bulldozer is just what you need to help clean up your room!

Tow-Truck Magnet

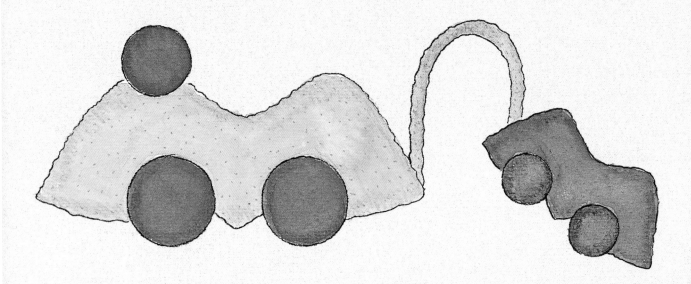

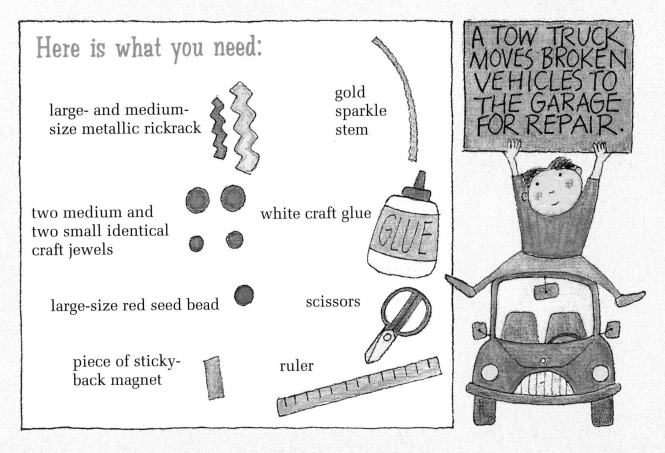

Here is what you need:

large- and medium-size metallic rickrack

gold sparkle stem

two medium and two small identical craft jewels

white craft glue

large-size red seed bead

scissors

piece of sticky-back magnet

ruler

A TOW TRUCK MOVES BROKEN VEHICLES TO THE GARAGE FOR REPAIR.

Here is what you do:

1. Cut two bumps from the large-size rickrack for the tow truck.

2. Cut two bumps from the medium-size rickrack for the car.

3. Glue the two medium craft jewels to the bottom of the larger piece of rickrack for wheels.

4. Glue the two smaller craft jewels to the medium piece of rickrack for wheels.

5. Glue the red seed bead to the top of the front bump of the tow truck for the flashing red light.

6. Cut a 2-inch (5-cm) piece of gold sparkle stem.

7. Trim the fibers of the sparkle stem as close to the wire as you can, to make it thinner.

8. Bend the sparkle stem. Glue one end of the sparkle stem to the bottom back of the tow truck and the other end to the front of the car. Adjust the sparkle stem so that the car is at an angle with the front wheels off the ground to look like it is being towed.

9. Press a piece of sticky-back magnet to the back of the tow truck.

Tow trucks have an important job!

Box Dump Truck

Here is what you need:

deep jewelry box with lid

smaller deep jewelry box with lid

ten twist ties, still attached to each other if, possible

two 12-inch (30-cm) pipe cleaners

scissors

white craft glue

ballpoint pen

marker

six plastic milk caps

DUMP TRUCKS ARE USED TO MOVE DIRT AND STONES TO OTHER PLACES.

Here is what you do:

1. Glue half of one end of the row of twist ties to one side of the top of the lid of the larger box.

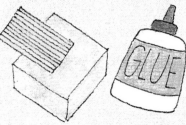

2. Glue the underside of the twist ties extending out from the lid to the edge of the bottom of the larger box. When the glue has dried, the box should fold down on top of the lid. The twist ties should serve as a hinge that allows the box to lie flat on top of the lid and tip back to dump a load.

3. Glue the smaller box to the lid of the larger box to form the cab of the truck. You may want to draw some windows and a windshield with a marker.

4. Use the ballpoint pen to poke a hole in the center of each milk cap.

5. Cut three 6-inch (15-cm) pieces of pipe cleaner for the wheel axles.

6. Use the ballpoint pen to poke a hole through the edge of the box on both sides at the front and back of the truck bed and through the bottom of the front cab of the truck.

7. Thread a piece of pipe cleaner through a milk cap, then through the holes on each side of the truck, then through another milk cap. Twist the ends of the pipe cleaner to the side to secure each wheel. Attach all three sets of wheels this way.

8. Use the pen to draw windows and add any other details you might want on your truck.

Try using the dump truck to move small stones, buttons, or some Legos. What else can you move with the dump truck?

Garbage Truck Scrap Collector

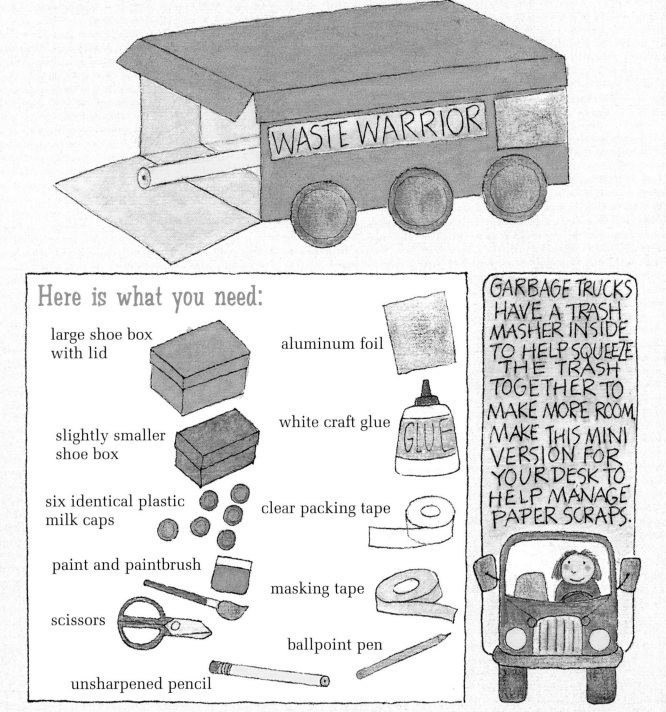

Here is what you need:

large shoe box with lid

slightly smaller shoe box

six identical plastic milk caps

paint and paintbrush

scissors

unsharpened pencil

aluminum foil

white craft glue

clear packing tape

masking tape

ballpoint pen

GARBAGE TRUCKS HAVE A TRASH MASHER INSIDE TO HELP SQUEEZE THE TRASH TOGETHER TO MAKE MORE ROOM. MAKE THIS MINI VERSION FOR YOUR DESK TO HELP MANAGE PAPER SCRAPS.

Here is what you do:

1. Cut down the two sides of one of the narrow ends of the larger shoe box to create a flap that will fold down.

2. Cut up the two side of one of the narrow ends of the lid to create a flap that folds up over the bottom flap. Place the lid on the box to become the truck body. Painting the truck body is optional.

3. Cut about one-fourth from one end of the smaller shoe box. (Save the lid and the leftover piece for another project.)

4. Use the clear packing tape to secure the eraser end of the pencil to the center of the bottom of the inside of the box.

5. Slip the flat side of the smaller box into the larger box through the back flap. This will be the "trash masher."

(continued on next page)

6. Tear a 3- by 12-inch (8- by 30-cm) strip of the aluminum foil for the windshield and windows of the truck.

7. Glue the strip across the front of the box with the ends wrapped around and glued to the two sides.

8. If the milk caps have tabs on the edge, use the scissors to snip them off.

9. Glue three milk caps along each side of the box for the wheels.

10. Use the ballpoint pen to write the name of the truck company on masking tape. Stick the masking tape sign to the side of the truck.

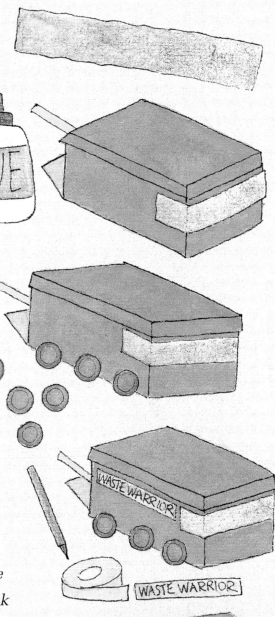

To use the truck, open the back flap and slide the "trash masher" out. Put scrap paper into the truck through the back and push it into the truck. Compress the scrap paper by pushing the pencil handle of the "trash masher."

Water-Squirting Fire Truck

Here is what you need:

red or yellow shoe box with lid (paint one if needed)

5-inch (13-cm)-square disposable food-saver container

empty, cleaned pump bottle such as soap comes in

8-ounce (227-g) plastic cup

construction paper

clear packing tape

aluminum foil

clamp clothespin

flexible plastic straw

white craft glue

scissors

hole punch

paper fastener

ruler

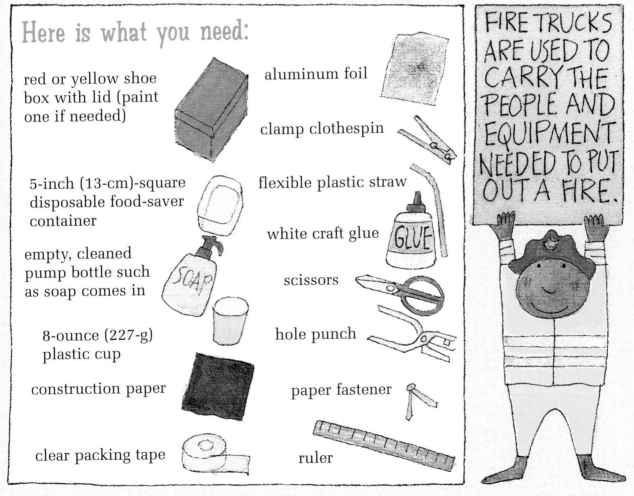

FIRE TRUCKS ARE USED TO CARRY THE PEOPLE AND EQUIPMENT NEEDED TO PUT OUT A FIRE.

(continued on next page)

Here is what you do:

1. Cut the lid of the shoe box in half, and save one-half for another project.

2. Cut a 3-inch (8-cm) slit in the top of each side of the lid. Fold the top flap up to create a windshield for the truck.

3. Cut a strip of aluminum foil, and glue it over the windshield. Cut a second strip, and glue it across the front of the box truck for a bumper.

4. Cut wheels from the construction paper. Glue the wheels on each side of the bottom part of the truck.

5. Punch a hole in the top of one side of the container.

6. Place the container in the back of the truck, and punch a second hole in the back of the truck. Join the container and the truck using a paper fastener.

7. Attach the plastic cup to the back of the container using the clamp clothespin.

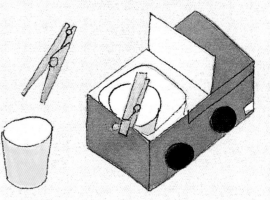

8. Use the packing tape to attach the bending end of the straw to the spout of the pump bottle.

9. Fill the bottle with water, and place the cap and straw back on.

10. Secure the pump bottle to the truck by placing it into the plastic cup. The "hose" can be aimed in different directions by bending it at the flex point. Push the pump to squirt water through the straw "hose."

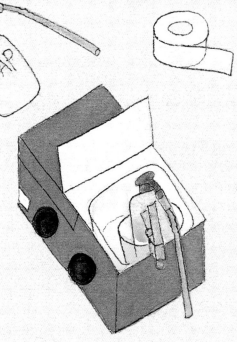

You might want to glue a paper door and windows to a square tissue box to make a house. Make some red, orange, and yellow marker lines on a tissue, and tuck it into the top of the box so that it looks like flames coming out of the roof of the house. Place the house on a washable floor, such as in the bathroom or kitchen or outside on the sidewalk. Slide the truck across the surface to the house, and "put out the fire" by pumping water on the tissue until it collapses and the fire is gone.

Snowplow Attachment

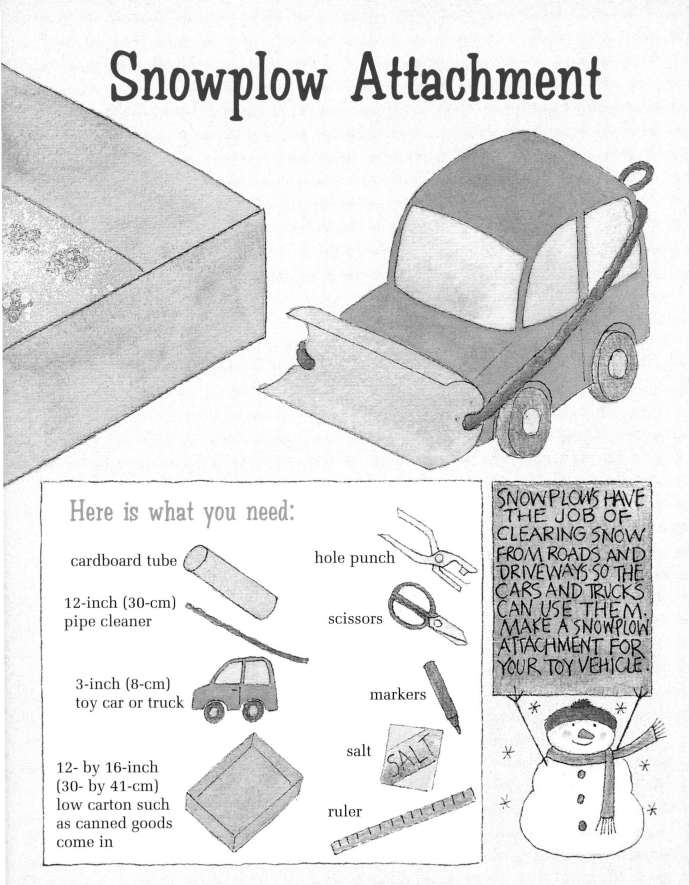

Here is what you need:

cardboard tube

12-inch (30-cm) pipe cleaner

3-inch (8-cm) toy car or truck

12- by 16-inch (30- by 41-cm) low carton such as canned goods come in

hole punch

scissors

markers

salt

ruler

SNOWPLOWS HAVE THE JOB OF CLEARING SNOW FROM ROADS AND DRIVEWAYS SO THE CARS AND TRUCKS CAN USE THEM. MAKE A SNOWPLOW ATTACHMENT FOR YOUR TOY VEHICLE.

Here is what you do:

1. Cut a 3-inch (8-cm) piece from one end of the cardboard tube.

2. Cut the piece in half, and use half for the scoop of the plow.

3. Punch a hole in the center of each edge of the cardboard plow.

4. Insert an end of the pipe cleaner through each of the holes in the plow. Twist the pipe cleaner around itself at each end to secure it to the plow.

5. Place the plow at the front of the truck with the pipe cleaner going around the truck.

6. Twist the pipe cleaner at the back of the truck to tighten it around the truck, and form a ring to use to move the plow up and down.

7. Using the markers, draw a town on the carton, with roads wide enough for the truck to drive on and plow.

8. Dump salt into the carton for snow. Use the snowplow to clear the snow from the road.

You might want to try using something else for the snow, such as cotton balls or white sand.

Tissue Box Bus

Here is what you need:

large-size cardboard tissue box

four 3-inch (8-cm)- empty ribbon spools

four erasers for pencil ends

two unsharpened pencils

scissors

clear packing tape

ballpoint pen

permanent marker

two paper fasteners

small rubber band

A BUS HAS ROOM FOR LOTS OF PEOPLE.

BUS STOP

Here is what you do:

1. Carefully pry open the seam on one side of the tissue box so that you have two flaps.

2. Turn the box on one side so the top opening becomes the bus window. If you wish, you can cut an identical window on the other side.

3. Cut another window at the front of the bus (the end of the tissue box).

4. Cover the window openings with clear packing tape on the outside and the inside, sticky sides together.

5. Use the pen to poke a hole through the bottom front and back of the bus for the wheel axles.

6. Push the pencils through the two holes at the front and back for the axles.

7. Put a ribbon spool on each end of the pencil axles, and secure them by placing an eraser over each pencil end. If the ribbon spools have writing on them, you might want to use the marker to cover the writing.

8. Put a paper fastener on the center edge of the two back flaps.

9. Slip the rubber band over one of the fastener heads. To close the door, slip the other end of the rubber band over the second fastener head.

10. Use the marker to give the bus a name.

"The wheels on the bus go round and round!"

Bead Train Necklace

Here is what you need:

ten ½-inch (1.3-cm) wooden beads

one smaller wooden bead

four pony beads

five matching pairs of small buttons

poster paints in black and four other colors and a paintbrush

yarn

Styrofoam tray to work on

12-inch (30-cm) red pipe cleaner

white craft glue

fiberfill

scissors

wood toothpick

ruler

LOTS OF PEOPLE OR THINGS CAN BE MOVED IN THE MANY CARS PULLED BY A TRAIN ENGINE.

Here is what you do:

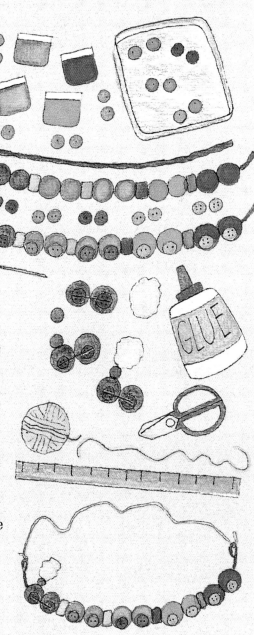

1. Working on the Styrofoam tray, paint the first two wooden beads and the small wooden bead black for the train engine.

2. Paint the remaining four pairs of wooden beads four different colors.

3. Let all the beads dry. Then string the sets of beads on the pipe cleaner with a pony bead in between each pair of beads.

4. Glue a pair of matching buttons to the bottom of each pair of beads for wheels.

5. Cut a 1½-inch (3.8-cm) piece of toothpick, and glue it across the engine wheels.

6. Glue the small black bead to the top of the front bead of the black engine to make the smokestack.

7. Glue a little bit of fiberfill in the top of the smokestack to look like smoke coming out.

8. Cut an 18-inch (46-cm) length of yarn.

9. Tie each end of the yarn to an end of the pipe cleaner to make a necklace. Fold the ends of the pipe cleaner over the tied yarn to secure.

Chuga-chuga, whoooooooooooo . . .

Bath Boat and Buddies

Here is what you need:

disposable
plastic cup

two or more dish
soap pull-spouts

clear packing tape

scissors

black permanent marker

Here is what you do:

1. Cut the cup in half, top to bottom.

2. Join the two halves of the cup at the rim, and secure with packing tape to make a simple boat.

3. Use the marker to draw faces and body details on the pull-spouts.

Float your boat!

TO TRAVEL ON WATER, YOU NEED A BOAT

Balloon Motorboat

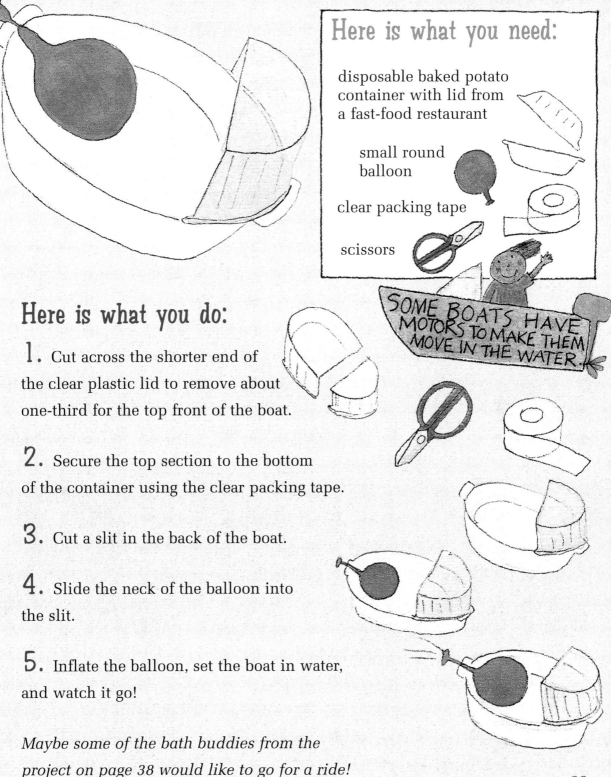

Here is what you need:

disposable baked potato container with lid from a fast-food restaurant

small round balloon

clear packing tape

scissors

Here is what you do:

1. Cut across the shorter end of the clear plastic lid to remove about one-third for the top front of the boat.

2. Secure the top section to the bottom of the container using the clear packing tape.

3. Cut a slit in the back of the boat.

4. Slide the neck of the balloon into the slit.

5. Inflate the balloon, set the boat in water, and watch it go!

Maybe some of the bath buddies from the project on page 38 would like to go for a ride!

SOME BOATS HAVE MOTORS TO MAKE THEM MOVE IN THE WATER.

Airplane Coming in for a Landing

Here is what you need:

16-ounce (454-g) plastic soda bottle

aluminum foil

poster board

sticker stars

two 1-inch (2.5-cm) buttons

plastic soda straw

clear packing tape

pipe cleaner

yarn or string

scissors

ruler

TO TRAVEL IN THE AIR YOU RIDE IN AN AIRPLANE.

Here is what you do:

1. Cut a 2- by 9-inch (5- by 23-cm) rectangle from the poster board. Round off the ends to make the wings for the airplane.

2. Decorate the wings with sticker stars. Then cover them with the clear packing tape.

3. Turn the bottle on one side. Use the tape to attach the wings to the top center of the bottle.

4. Cover the bottle and the center part of the wings with aluminum foil. Decorate the plane with more sticker stars.

5. Cut a 4-inch (10-cm) piece of pipe cleaner.

6. Attach a button to each end of the pipe cleaner piece by threading the ends through the holes.

7. Use the packing tape to attach the center of the pipe cleaner to the bottom of the airplane. Bend the two wheels down on each side of the tape.

8. Cut a 2-inch (5-cm) piece of plastic straw. Tape the piece of straw to the top of the airplane between the wings.

9. Cut a 12-foot (3.7-m) piece of string or yarn for the plane to slide on.

10. Thread one end of the yarn through the straw at the top of the airplane.

To fly the plane in for a landing, have one person hold the end of the string close to the floor while you hold the opposite end up higher. Slide the plane down the string to come in for a landing.

Helicopter Puppet

Here is what you need:

Styrofoam egg

red permanent marker

aluminum foil

white craft glue

four silver sparkle stems

two paper fasteners

small pom-pom

two wiggle eyes

scissors

corrugated cardboard

ruler

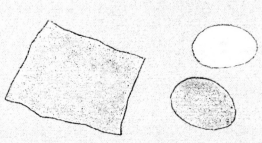

A HELICOPTER CAN GO STRAIGHT UP IN THE AIR AND DOWN AGAIN.

Here is what you do:

1. Cover the Styrofoam egg with aluminum foil to make the body of the helicopter.

2. Give the helicopter a face by gluing the wiggle eyes and pom-pom nose to the wide end of the egg shape. Use the marker to draw a smile.

3. Shape a propeller for the helicopter by folding a sparkle stem into three or four loops and bending the end down to push it into the top of the helicopter.

4. Shape a smaller two-blade propeller from a piece of sparkle stem, and insert it in the back of the helicopter.

5. Bend both arms of the two paper fasteners to one side and press the ends into the bottom of the helicopter, side by side, for the wheels.

6. Twist two sparkle stems together, and press the end into the bottom of the helicopter behind the wheels for a handle for the puppet.

7. Cut a 5-inch (13-cm) square of corrugated cardboard for the landing pad.

8. Poke a hole in the center of the cardboard, and push the handle of the puppet down through the hole so that the helicopter rests on the landing pad.

To use the puppet, push up on the handle to make the helicopter take off, spin, and come back down.

43

Secret Message Rocket Ships

Here is what you need:

two fat marker caps

two self-stick pin backs

gold and red sparkle stems

scrap paper

aluminum foil

pen

scissors

star stickers

ruler

TO TRAVEL TO OUTER SPACE, YOU NEED A ROCKET SHIP.

Here is what you do:

1. To make each of the two rocket ships, tear off a 12- by 4-inch (30- by 10-cm) strip of aluminum foil.

2. Fold the strip in half, side to side, so it is 6 by 4 inches (15 by 10 cm).

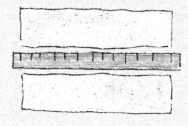

3. Place a marker cap on the foil with the open end of the cap about 1/4-inch (.6 cm) from the end. Roll the cap inside the foil to cover it.

4. Tuck the ¼-inch of excess foil at the open end of the cap inside the opening.

5. Squeeze the top foil into a point to form the top of the rocket ship. Trim off the excess foil.

6. Stick a star on the front of the rocket ship and a pin back on the back.

7. Cut a 6-inch (15-cm) piece of sparkle stem in both red and gold.

8. Fold the red stem in half. Cut the gold stem in half. Insert the sparkle stems into the open end of the rocket ship to look like fire coming out of the bottom.

9. Cut squares of scrap paper to fit inside the rocket ship. The notes can be rolled around the end of the sparkle stems before being inserted into the cap. To make it easier to remove the message, bend the tip of one of the cut stems over the edge of the note so that when the stems are removed the note will come with them.

Give one rocket ship to a friend. By trading ships, you can pass secret notes to each other. No one will suspect the rocket ships really carry secret messages.

Design-a-Vehicle Tin

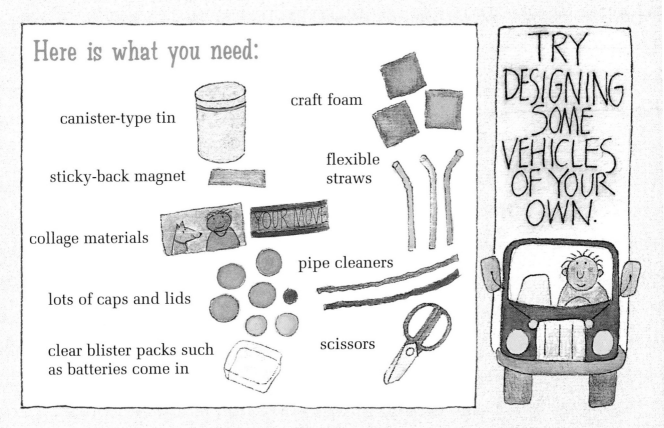

Here is what you need:

canister-type tin

craft foam

sticky-back magnet

flexible straws

collage materials

lots of caps and lids

pipe cleaners

clear blister packs such as batteries come in

scissors

TRY DESIGNING SOME VEHICLES OF YOUR OWN.

Here is what you do:

1. Make an endless number of different vehicles by using pieces of sticky-back magnet to attach various parts to the outside of the tin.

2. The caps and lids make great wheels, headlights, and sirens.

3. Use the blister packs as windshields and windows.

4. Thread a pipe cleaner through a straw to make a tow bar.

5. Cut fins and other trims from craft foam.

This is a project that can be added to over time as you choose new vehicles to make and create the parts needed from collage materials. You can store all the pieces inside the tin.

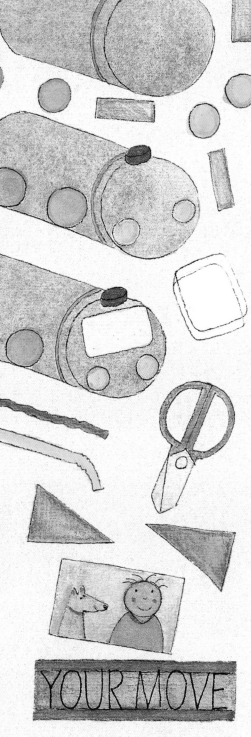

YOUR MOVE

About the Author and Artist

Thirty years as a teacher and director of nursery school programs have given Kathy Ross extensive experience in guiding young children through crafts projects. Among the more than forty craft books she has written are **_Crafts for All Seasons_, _More of the Best Holiday Crafts Ever_, _The Storytime Craft Book_**, and the **_All New Holiday Crafts for Kids_** series. You can find out more about Kathy's books by visiting her at www.Kathyross.com

Jan Barger, originally from Little Rock, Arkansas, now lives in Plumpton, East Sussex, England, with her husband and their cocker spaniel, Tosca. She has written and illustrated a number of children's books and is known for her gentle humor and warm, friendly characters. She also designs greeting cards, sings with the Brighton Festival Chorus, and plays piccolo with the Sinfonia of Arun.

Together, Kathy and Jan have written and illustrated two earlier volumes in this series, **_Crafts for Kids Who Are Learning about Community Workers_** and **_Crafts for Kids Who Are Learning about Weather_**, as well as the **_Learning Is Fun_** series.